Healing,

While Walking in Your Purpose

TONYA BAILEY

Healing, While Walking in Your Purpose

Tonya Bagwell-Bailey

Healing, While Walking in Your Purpose

Scripture quotations are taken from the Holy Bible, King James Version (KJV) Copyright © 2003 by Thomas Nelson, Inc. Used by permission. All rights reserved.

God Purpose for Your Life (with commentary). *James Wilson* June 25, 2025

Walk in Your Purpose- A Step-by-Step Guide (that works). *Daniel-Prayer Warrior.* May 10, 2023, updated January 23, 2024

Walking in Your Worth: The Significance of Discovering One's Purpose. *Dominique M. Williams* October 31. 2024

Biblical Meaning of Weakness: Embracing God's Strength in Our Struggles. *Christine Blanchard* March 22, 2025

Printed in the United States of America

ISBN: 979-8-9942906-2-0

Published by Grace 4 Purpose, Publishing Co. LLC

www.grace4purpose.com

Dedication

This book is dedicated to all who have faced—or are currently facing—challenges in their lives.

Table of Contents

"True healing begins from within and requires patience, humility, and trust in God's timing."

Chapter I
What is Healing

What Healing Feels Like

*H*ave you ever wondered what healing really means? Healing is a process of becoming healthy and whole again. It feels like being set free — from pain, people, or the troubles of life. Healing is like having a weight lifted off your shoulders. It's that moment when the rain stops, the clouds open, and the sun peaks through with a rainbow to follow. Suddenly, you can breathe again.

Our bodies, mind and souls are tender. It takes a lot of courage and intention to heal from sickness, trauma, or hurt. Healing isn't just about feeling better; it's about letting go and finding freedom.

The Process of Healing

Healing takes time. It may take weeks, months, or even years depending on what you're healing from. Life has a way of knocking us off our feet, and often without warning. Whether the wound is physical, emotional, mental, or even financial, healing goes deeper than surface-level comfort.

Think about a surgery: the outside may look closed and healed, but inside the tissue is still tender. That's why true healing begins from within. It requires patience, humility, and trust in God's timing.

God's Role in Our Healing

Healing requires faith. It's about trusting and believing God will carry you through. Scripture reminds us:

- *"Now set your mind and heart to seek the Lord your God."* - 1 Chronicles 22:19

- *"My grace is sufficient for you, for my power is made perfect in weakness."* - 2 Corinthians 12:9

- *"Count it all joy when you meet trials of various kinds."* - James 1:2-4

Sometimes healing involves suffering, frustration, or waiting. We don't always like the process, but God will keep us in a season until He sees fit to move us forward. He wants us to learn, grow, and recognize that we are not meant to remain in broken spaces.

That is why prayer, daily time in His Word, and surrendering to His will are essential. Healing comes when we allow God to work within us.

The Challenges Along the Way

Healing isn't easy. You may feel bound by relationships, generational curses, or financial struggles. Just when you think you've broken free, something else tries to pull you back in. That's why healing requires strength, commitment, and dedication. You must be willing to change, accept truth, and move forward even when it's uncomfortable.

Our weaknesses remind us how much we need God. They push us into His presence and open the door for personal growth. God's strength shines brightest when we surrender our limitations to Him.

Rest and Restoration

Healing also requires rest —physically and spiritually. Physical rest restores your strength. Spiritual rest brings peace and draws you closer to God.

In those quiet moments of prayer, meditation, and gratitude, your faith deepens. God is not only able to heal, but also to restore. He can rebuild the years that were lost, mend broken hearts, and restore everything the enemy has stolen.

Dear God,

I ask you to grant us the knowledge to know what it means to be healed, and to have the strength to endure whatever trial comes our way. Teach us to not be so careful to let our issues overpower our minds.

In Jesus' Name, Amen.

"Healing begins when we are honest about how we arrived here and willing to walk it out with patience."

Chapter II
Understanding Your Healing

Accepting and Acknowledging the Issue

*T*o understand our healing, we must first accept and acknowledge the issue. We have to be honest about how we arrived at this place, be willing to work through it, and be patient as we walk it out. Healing begins when we recognize the emotions, thoughts, and behaviors connected to our struggles.

Healing isn't only about recovering from sickness. Sometimes it's about understanding why we feel stagnant, why we keep attracting the same people, or why we feel stuck in life. Often, it is because we are trying to remain in a moment God is calling us out of.

"Draw nigh to God, and he will draw nigh to you." – James 4:8 (KJV)

Choosing God Over the World

We often get caught up in the world, following the crowd, doing what feels good in the moment, and settling into habits that harm us in the long run. Once we get comfortable, it gets difficult to let those things go. That is why having a real relationship with God is so important. He is the one who can move us out of unhealthy places and set us on the right path.

"But seek ye first the kingdom of God, and his righteous; and all these things shall be added unto you." **Matthew 6:33 (KJV)**

The Cost of Understanding Our Healing

Understand that healing comes with sacrifice and sometimes being placed in uncomfortable situations. God will allow us to go through seasons of stretching so that we can grow. We must be willing to fight through the pain to come out stronger.

We all have different journeys, but no matter what ours looks like, the answer remains the same: rely on the One who created us. God promises never to leave or forsake us. Standing on His Word will help us understand and endure the healing process.

Practical Steps Toward Healing

True healing begins on the inside. That's where we often hide our hurt, pain, trauma and disappointment. Healing means remembering who we are beneath the layers of trauma, stress, generational curses, physical hurt, and emotional wounds.

When we embrace freedom, our testimony can inspire others who are still struggling. We strengthen our healing by treating ourselves with kindness and practicing self-compassion. Healing is not about fighting ourselves, or anyone else; it's about allowing God to shape who He has called us to be.

"He heals the brokenhearted and binds up their wounds" – *Psalm 147:3 (NIV)*

Progress, Not Perfection

Healing is not about perfection, it's about progress. It's about patience and trusting God to bring the change we need. Comparing our journey to someone else's only leads to discouragement. Our story is unique, and God is using it in His way and timing.

Living With Intention

Understanding our healing means living intentionally. We must align with our values, set goals, and make room for joy. Our healing journey will include ups and downs, but we should celebrate every small step forward.

True understanding comes when we can show up as our authentic selves, without masks or pretense. Even when we smile through pain, that smile may become the reason someone else finds hope. Sometimes our journey isn't just for us; it is for others to witness God's power at work in our lives.

A Shift in Mindset

Understanding our healing means shifting our mindset. We must choose to turn from negative thoughts to positive ones. We must choose growth. We must choose to walk boldly in what God has ordained for us.

"Be transformed by the renewing of your mind..." – Romans 12:2 (NIV)

Dear God,

I come to you asking you for understanding of what it truly means to be healed. Guide us when we feel overwhelmed and out of alignment with You. Teach us to trust you with our healing process.

In Jesus' Name, Amen.

"Stop hiding behind silence—release the hurt and let God lead you forward."

Chapter III
Healing from Your Hurts

Healing Starts From Within

*A*s I stated earlier, healing takes place from inside the out. Healing often hurts, because it requires confronting and processing painful emotions and experiences that have been suppressed or avoided. To heal, you must acknowledge the hurt and go through it.

There are many ways to express pain: journaling, mindfulness, setting healthy boundaries, or speaking to a professional. Hurt can come from suffering, trauma, sickness, or loss. Each experience weighs differently on us, often leaving anxiety, heaviness, or emotional vulnerability behind.

But even in suffering, you cannot dwell in it. You must keep moving, because trouble does not last always.

Physical Healing Requires Obedience and Rest

When healing from physical illness or pain, rest and proper care are essential. Think about cancer, it has a major impact on individuals and families because the body goes through so much just to keep going. Many feel like their life is over when they hear the diagnosis, but it doesn't have to be.

When you tap into your source, and seek God, and believe that He will heal you, you walk through even the darkest valleys with hope.

Heal me, Oh Lord, and I shall be healed: save me, and I shall be saved, for you are my praise. Jeremiah 17:14 (KJV)

Healing From Generational and Emotional Trauma

Trauma from generational curses, childhood experiences, or adulthood pain will continue to hurt until it is addressed. Many of us were taught to "be quiet," "don't talk about it," or "just deal with it." But suppressed pain grows heavier over time.

Healing often begins with releasing the hurt:

- Talking about the trauma

- Breaking generational cycles

- Refusing to repeat patterns taught years ago

- Confessing sins

- Admitting wrongdoings

- Forgiving yourself so you can truly be forgiven

. Breaking generational curses may cause separation or conflict within families, but peace is worth the sacrifice. Stop hiding behind secrets, excuses, and silence. Let it go, and let God give you the courage to move forward.

Healing Through Grief and Loss

Healing from death can take days, months or even years. Some of us are grieving deeply, and yes, it is hard. People grieve differently, and that is okay. We are not meant to feel the same or grieve the same.

Death does not have a timeline. We all have felt it's sting and will one day face it ourselves. Yet Scripture reminds us: *Isaiah 35:10* *"Earth has no sorrow that heaven cannot heal."- Isaiah 35:10 (KJV)*

To me, "no sorrow" means freedom, letting go, trusting God, and allowing Him to comfort us. When a loved one dies, their spirit returns to God, and their physical body returns to the ground from which we were formed.

Healing from grief doesn't have to look pretty. Don't paint over it; let it be what it is. Your healing may feel messy, exhausting, or overwhelming, but healing still comes.

Healing From Collective Trauma-A Look Back at 2019

About five years ago, the world experienced a moment that changed us all: COVID 19. It was a "what-if" moment that touched every part of our lives. The world was not prepared for it, nor did we understand where it came from. Overnight, everything shifted.

Life took us in a collective journey:

- Staying inside for weeks

- Scaling back daily routines

- Empty shelves and limited supplies

- Lost jobs and reduced incomes

- Families forced to face unresolved issues

- Many grieving unexpected loss

Sadly, many lost loved ones, but even in that, it was God's timing. For those who survived, God still has a purpose and a plan for your life.

Healing from that season continues today. Some are still recovering financially, emotionally, and spiritually. Some are still rebuilding their health or grieving their losses. Healing from collective trauma takes time.

But God remains the answer. He can heal, restore, and set you free. When you trust and never doubt, God will show up and show out.

Letting God Lead You Through the Hurt

Living in a world where many believe they can operate without God is dangerous. COVID-19 reminded us all that we need Him. God got this country's attention and slowed everything down so we could reflect, pray, reset and return to Him.

Dear God,

I ask you to grant us your grace and mercy as we go through the process of healing from our hurts. Allow us to release these hurts over to you and not to go back to them and start afresh. Lord, guide us in the way we should go and let us not fret to fall short.

In Jesus' Name, Amen.

"Healing is a daily decision—just as we once chose cycles, we must now choose freedom."

Chapter IV
Are We Really Healed?

What Healing Really Looks Like

How do you know if we are healed or not? Healing is not always warm and fuzzy. Sometimes it feels dark, confusing, and full of twists and turns. At times, God will even lead us back to old situations so we can confront the things we once avoided in order to truly heal. It may not make sense to us, but in God's plan, it fits perfectly.

When it feels worse before it feels better, that is often a sign that healing is taking place. It means we are finally touching the parts of ourselves we have once denied. Healing is a daily decision. Throughout the day, we may need to remind ourselves that we are choosing healing. Just as we once chose cycles and struggles, we must now choose freedom and wholeness.

Healing happens in small steps. It shows up in the little behavioral changes that add up over time. Everyone's healing journey is different, and the timing is not the same for all of us. Healing is a journey, not a destination. Along the way there may be setbacks, delays, or disappointments, but we must remember that we are strong and mighty in God.

Facing Ourselves

The question we may ask is: **"Am I really healed?"**

The truth is, we are not healed if we are still in the same place, connected to the same people, and unwilling to press forward. Many of us cope by distracting ourselves, appearing strong on the outside, while hurting on the inside.

At some point, we must decide to make a change so we can see life differently and allow ourselves to heal.

Have we ever considered that sometimes the source of our pain is not someone else but ourselves? We often blame others before taking an honest look at our own patterns. Self-reflection is a powerful tool. It helps us identify our faults, acknowledge our growth, and understand our emotions. It allows us to make sense of what we are feeling and how we can move forward.

Depending on God

As one songwriter once said, *"God wants to heal you everywhere you hurt."* That is His desire for us. God wants us to depend on Him, and not remain stuck in the same space. When we pray sincerely, bringing our needs, desires, and weaknesses before Him, He responds with power, grace, and mercy.

Christ gave His life not only so we could have eternal life, but so we could grow, persevere, and be restored while we live here on earth.

Signs of True Healing

We know healing is happening when we feel safe within ourselves, when we feel connected, and when we can be fully present in the moment. Healing builds resilience, strength, wisdom and determination. It gives us confidence to face life boldly.

You will know you are healed when you can revisit situations without feeling overwhelmed.

Some tools that can help in the healing process are:

- Speak positive affirmations
- Praying
- Reading and meditating on God's Word
- Walking and exercising
- Talking to a trusted professional.

When the healing comes, humility is essential. We cannot forget where we once were. Healing is not complete if we devote all our energy to the world but little to God. We must be willing to let go, even let go of ourselves, so that God can fully heal us.

Jesus said: ***"Come to me, all of you who are weary and carry heavy burdens, and I will give you rest…. For my yoke is easy to*** *bear, and the burden I you give is light." -***Matthew 11:28-29**

(NLT)

True healing is not about avoiding pain but facing it with courage, while learning how to lean on God in the process.

Walking in Freedom

Pain, suffering, trauma, and generational curses are not our sanctuary, **God is our sanctuary**. When we allow these things to linger, they keep us feeling unhealed and bound. We have one life to live, and it should be lived free from pain, regret and negative strongholds.

Growth and healing work hand in hand. As we heal, our walk changes, our outlook brightens, and our faith deepens. The question, "Are you really healed?" does not have to stay linger. Healing comes when we release what is holds us back, surrender control to God, and walk boldly in the purpose He has designed for us.

He wants us to prosper and be intentional about Him. If God were

to ask you today, **"Do you want to be healed?"** what would be

your response be?

Dear God,

I am asking you to allow us to seek You on this healing journey. Grant us wisdom, direction and discernment to know when it is time to step away from things that do not align with You. Help us to trust You with our whole hearts and surrender what we've been holding onto.

In Jesus' Name, Amen

"We were never meant to become someone else—purpose flows from who God created us to be."

Chapter V
Walking in Your Purpose

Living in Alignment With God's Will

When we walk in our purpose, we are living in alignment with God's will for our lives, our values, our goals, and our destiny. Our actions should reflect our beliefs. Some may ask, *"How can I walk in my purpose, with* what I am going through?"

The answer is simple: **God**. He has a divine purpose and plan for each one of us.

In our walk, we should feel joy and yield to love others. Walking in our purpose allows us to serve God and remain open to what He desires for us. It is important to create structure, stay on track, and still make space for rest. As we yield to the Holy Spirit, we begin to see God's plan and purpose for our lives unfold before us, and we will be able to step into our purpose unfold before us, and we step into it with confidence and faith.

Surrendering to His Plan

God wants us to surrender our desires and follow His plan. With so many distractions in the world, it can be difficult to discern our purpose. But when we seek guidance from the Highest, He will reveal our gifts, talents, and the assignment connected to our lives.

When we are not walking in our purpose, we chase pleasures and look for validation from others. We lose sight of our worth, worship material things and follow the crowd. But when we God's purpose, we gain direction and stability in our daily lives.

"Trust in the Lord with all thine heart; and lean not unto thine own understanding; in all thy ways acknowledge him, and he shall direct thy path."- **Proverbs 3:5-6**

Uniquely Created

Each of us was created with unique talents, strengths, and passions designed to serve God and others. Understanding our purpose helps us show up fully in our communities and express God's love in practical, impactful ways.

God created each of us differently. We can never become someone else, nor should we try. Purpose is not found by following the footsteps of others, but following the direction of God.

When we walk in purpose, we leave a legacy that reflects God's love, intention, and glory. His desire is for us to live a life pleasing to Him and meaningful to others.

Progress is Progression

Purpose is not about perfection, it is about continuous progression as we discover who we are beyond the masks, wounds, and past experiences. That is why patience and persistence are essential.

Walking in our purpose is not easy and is not for the faint of heart. Challenges and obstacles will arise, but with faith, determination, and the guidance of the Holy Spirit, we can overcome anything and fulfill God's calling for our lives.

Timing is everything. We should not be discouraged by how long the journey takes. God's timing is perfect, and His plans are greater than we can imagine.

Embrace this time season of growth. Allow the Holy Spirit to reveal the calling that only you can fulfill. You will be amazed at the great things God has prepared for you.

Walking Boldly in Purpose

To walk in your purpose, you must step out on faith, pray, study the Word, listen to the voice of God, and release your own plans and desires. Surround yourself with individuals who align with God's will and uplift your spiritual walk.

When we understand, accept and heal from our hurts, God invites us to walk in purpose. Surrendering to Him and giving Him our "yes" is all He asks. Our purpose is to glorify God and build a relationship with Him.

As we walk in our purpose, opportunities will arise that is align with our assignment and lead to greater abundance. We will recognize our worth and guard our spirit from anything that seeks to disrupt our walk.

Purpose brings clarity, resilience, and transformation. Those who once knew us will no longer see the old version of us, but the light and change God has placed within us.

Staying the Course

Purpose is your guide. It elevates, heals, and empowers us to live the life we were created for. It brings peace and hope, confirming that we are aligned with God's plan.

Stepping into purpose does not mean we returning to old ways. It means moving forward, choosing what is right, and trusting God's direction. Our desires mirror others, but God gives each of us our own dreams and visions so we can prosper according to His will.

Our walk should exemplify God and the light within us. As long as we seek His direction, we will not be misled. His purpose for us is to love Him with all our heart, mind, body and soul, and love our neighbors as ourselves.

Every season has a reason. To step into the new, we must release the old. Purpose leads us to a better life, but distractions can cause us to miss what God is revealing. It is time to get in position and be ready to **WALK IN YOUR PURPOSE.**

Dear God,

I come with all I have asking you to grant me grace to understand the purpose You have ordained within me. Allow me to walk in my purpose without judgement, and show up as a vessel of you. God allow my light to shine so that all people can see you through me.

In Jesus' Name, Amen

Author Tonya Bagwell-Bailey

About the Author

Tonya Bagwell-Bailey is a devoted wife, a woman of resilience, and someone passionate about being a blessing to others. As an award-winning author, she shares her testimonies of her healing in her books, captivating the hearts and minds of readers around the world.

Tonya resides on the Eastern Shore of Virginia with her husband, Craig. She holds a bachelor's degree in Health Management/Administration and an MBA. She is the author of *Pray Without Ceasing, Vision and Goal Planner,* and the co-author of *Fatih While Waiting.*

In addition to her literary accomplishments, Tonya is a passionate podcaster. She hosts two shows: *Journey of a Kidney Survivor and Pushing to your Purpose, where* she shares her journey as a transplant recipient, breast cancer survivor, and how to keep pressing forward through life's challenges.

Faith has always been the cornerstone of Tonya's life, especially during her health challenges. She is an active member the Shiloh Baptist Church, where she serves as a Deaconess and participates in both the Decoration and Outreach ministries. Tonya finds peace in knowing that God is faithful and fulfills His promises.

Her work has been featured in *Speak Up Sis, Black Women Author, and Unmasking Motivation* magazines, as well as on *The Happy Entrepreneur Show* with *Che Brown* and in *Author's Impact Hub*. Beyond being an author, Tonya is also a professional life coach, speaker, and advocate for chronic illness.

Contact Information

Email: www.tonya.bailey89@yahoo.com

Website: www.tonyabagwell-bailey.com

Facebook: Tonya B Bailey

Instagram: @tonya_b_bailey

Additional Books

Pray Without Ceasing

Vision and Goal Planner

Fatih While Waiting

www.grace4purposeco.com